Food in Art

in

Art

ROSEMARY MOORE

Wayland

LOOKING AT ART

Animals in Art
Faces in Art
Food in Art
Water in Art

Looking at Art is based on the *Discovering Art* series by Christopher McHugh, published by Wayland (Publishers) Ltd in 1992.

Cover: top left *Winter* by Giuseppe Arcimboldo, top right *Still Life with Jug and Fruit* by Paul Cézanne, bottom left *The Buckwheat Harvest* by Emile Bernard, bottom right Fruit and vase - Roman still life.

Editor: Deborah Elliott
Designer: Malcolm Walker
Cover design: Simon Balley

First published in 1995 by
Wayland (Publishers) Ltd.
61 Western Road, Hove
East Sussex BN3 1JD

British Library Cataloguing in Publication Data
Moore, Rosemary
  Food in Art - (Looking at Art Series)
  I. Title II. Series
704.9496413

ISBN 0-7502-1439-2

Typeset by Kudos, England
Printed and bound in Italy by G.Canale & C.S.p.A., Turin

Contents

Food in painting   4

Food in ancient times   6

Food for rich and poor   9

Food in different countries   12

Food in the Middle Ages   16

Still life paintings   18

Bread and meat   22

Food and drink   24

Who are the artists?   28

Glossary   30

Books to read   31

About the pictures   31

Index   32

Food in painting

Because food is one of the most important things in most people's lives, artists have always liked to make pictures showing different kinds of food and people eating meals.

This picture of people having a meal was painted by an Italian artist called Caravaggio. It shows Jesus Christ having a meal with some of his followers, called disciples. Jesus is the figure in the middle at the back.

▼ *Supper at Emmaus* by Caravaggio, in the National Gallery in London.

▲ *Winter* by Giuseppe Arcimboldo. Private collection.

There are lots of different fruits and vegetables in this painting. How many can you count? Can you also see that the pile of vegetables on the right forms the shape of a man? His hat is a cauliflower and his beard is a type of lettuce. He wears a cloak made of pears, apples and other fruits, with a large bunch of celery hanging over his shoulder. The artist called this picture *Winter*. Can you guess why?

Food in ancient times

▲ An Ancient Egyptian painting, now in the British Museum in London.

Both pictures on this page were made in Ancient Egypt, over 5,000 years ago. Above is a picture made on a kind of paper called papyrus. It shows a farmer ploughing a field ready for sowing seeds. Below, servants are working in a kitchen preparing ducks for roasting.

◄ A kitchen scene, painted on the wall of a tomb in the ancient city of Thebes in Egypt.

Below is a picture painted on the side of a large vase. It was made in Ancient Greece, about 2,000 years later than the Egyptian paintings opposite.

The picture shows two Greek goddesses called Demeter and Persephone. Can you see them on either side of the messenger, who is sitting in a winged chariot? The goddesses are giving the messenger gifts of wheat and wine to take to the people on Earth.

Demeter was the Greek goddess of farming and she was believed to have the power to provide good or bad harvests for the people on Earth. Persephone was Demeter's daughter.

A vase showing a scene from an Ancient Greek story. It is in the British Museum in London. ▶

The pictures on this page come from Ancient Rome. They both show wealthy Romans eating a meal. The top picture was painted on a wall and shows a group of people chatting together happily while servants bring food.

The bottom picture is a type of sculpture called a relief. These Romans are also enjoying a very good meal.

▲ A wall painting from Pompeii and a Roman relief sculpture. ▼

Food for rich and poor

▲ *Peasant Wedding* by Pieter Brueghel the Elder. This painting is in the Kunsthistorisches Museum in Vienna.

This picture was painted by an artist in Belgium about 500 years ago. It shows many people enjoying a wedding feast. Everybody is having a good time and there is lots to eat and drink.

▲ *La Chasse* by Charles van Loo. It is in a private collection.

The pictures on these two pages show very different types of people eating very different kinds of meal. Above we see rich people picnicking in the country. These were aristocrats, who lived in France over 200 years ago, at a time when the rich were very rich indeed, and the poor suffered terrible hardships and poverty. These lucky people have come to a beautiful place in the countryside, to be served a delicious meal by servants.

The painting on this page was made by an artist who died just over 100 years ago. His name was Vincent van Gogh, and this is one of his early paintings. It shows a group of poor farm workers having a meal which consisted only of potatoes and cups of tea. Van Gogh has used dark colours to show the gloom and poverty of the people, unlike the rich, bright colours of the picnic opposite.

▼ *The Potato Eaters* by Vincent van Gogh. This painting is in the Van Gogh Museum in Amsterdam.

Food in different countries

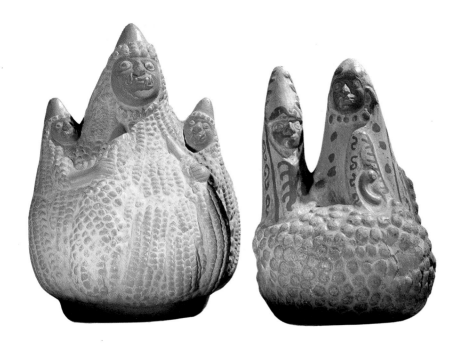

◀ Maize goddesses made by the Mochica people of South America. They are 1,500 years old.

On the next four pages we see how artists have shown different kinds of food in countries all over the world. Some of the pictures show foods that mean something important to people, and others show special or festive meals.

The two clay pots above are in the shape of corn cobs. The pots were made many centuries ago by people called the Mochicas, who lived in the part of South America we now call Peru. Maize, or Indian corn, was a very important food for the Mochicas and their maize goddesses were among the most highly regarded of their gods.

▶ A Navaho woven blanket. It is in a private collection in New York.

This blanket with a picture woven into it was made by the Navaho people of North America. Like the Mochica people, the Navaho also enjoyed eating maize and prized it very highly. The woven picture shows a tall maize plant. On each side of the maize plant are figures that show different spirits of nature, including the spirits of rain and thunder.

The picture on the left comes from Australia. It is a bark painting made by an Aboriginal artist. The artist drew the picture on tree bark, using pointed sticks and paints made from different coloured earth and rocks. The picture shows two fish, which the Aboriginal people may sometimes eat.

◀ An Aboriginal bark painting showing two fish.

▲ *A Banquet and Concert* in the Palace Museum in Taipei.

This picture was painted on silk. It comes from Ancient China and is very old. The picture shows a group of rich people dining at the Emperor's palace. Because the painting is so old and delicate, it is quite difficult to make out what the people are eating. But we can see the comfortable stools they are sitting on, and the little dog crouched under the table, perhaps waiting for titbits.

The painting on the right comes from Persia, which we now call Iran. It shows lots of people preparing a meal. One man is pouring water into a pot, another is cutting up meat and a woman is mixing dough. At the bottom of the picture are the creatures which will soon go into the cooking pots.

The picture below, of women enjoying a meal, was made by a Japanese artist, about 100 years ago.

▲ A Persian manuscript painting in the Teheran Museum in Iran.

► A twentieth-century Japanese print, in the Victoria and Albert Museum, London.

Food in the Middle Ages

The pictures on these pages come from the Middle Ages. On the right are scenes from an old French calendar. They show the months of July and August, when the corn was harvested.

▲ Part of an old calendar painted in France in about AD 1200.

The picture below shows a story from the Bible, when Jesus Christ, with his mother Mary and a disciple, were invited to a wedding feast. When the wine ran out, Jesus performed a miracle by turning water into wine.

◄ *The Marriage at Cana*, a manuscript painting made by monks in about AD 1200.

▲ An illustration from a French story *The Romance of Renaud de Montauban*, painted in the fifteenth century.

The picture above was also painted in the Middle Ages and shows people at a banquet. As in the wedding picture opposite, the important people are shown much bigger than the servants. The three women at the middle table are obviously noblewomen. They are beautifully dressed and appear much larger than the men sitting at the table on the right.

Still life paintings

The pictures in this chapter are all of things that do not move, so they are called 'still lifes'. Artists have always liked to paint pictures of fruit or other food, usually on a table, ready to be eaten. The still life below was painted by a Roman artist. It is about 2,000 years old.

▼ A wall painting found buried under volcanic ash at Pompeii in Italy.

▲ *Breakfast Still Life with a Crab* by Pieter Claesz. The picture is in a private collection.

The still life above was painted much more recently – about 400 years ago, in The Netherlands. Although the artist has made the food look very real, he has also made the picture look interesting and attractive. Notice the vine leaves at the back, and how he has shown the light reflected on the glasses and the shadows of the folded tablecloth.

▲ *Still Life with Jug and Fruit* by Paul Cézanne. This painting is in the National Gallery in Oslo, Norway.

The still lifes on these two pages were both painted at the end of the last century by French artists. The picture above is by Paul Cézanne. He has used strong, clear colours and bold brush strokes to show the light shining on the apples and oranges, and on the jug.

The still life below was painted by Paul Gauguin, who was a friend of Cézanne. Although early in his career Gauguin lived and painted in France, he later went to live on an island in the Pacific Ocean. There he painted many pictures of the islanders and the food they ate. This picture shows mangoes, which are tropical fruits.

▼ *Still Life with Mangoes* by Paul Gauguin. This picture is in a private collection.

Bread and meat

The picture below was painted by an artist working in The Netherlands over three hundred years ago. His name was Jan Vermeer and he especially liked to paint pictures of ordinary people doing everyday jobs. This picture shows a young woman in her kitchen.

◀ *The Maid with a Milk Jug* by Jan Vermeer. This painting is in the Rijksmuseum in Amsterdam.

The two pictures on this page are not for vegetarians! They both show large amounts of meat. The huge carcass on the right was painted by Rembrandt who, like Vermeer, lived in The Netherlands. Rembrandt shows the flesh and bones of an ox as it hangs in a butcher's shop, ready to be sold.

▲ *The Flayed Ox* by Rembrandt. You can see this picture in the Glasgow City Art Gallery.

Below is a painting by the English artist William Hogarth. He often painted pictures telling a story. This one shows a scene in a French town, at a time when England and France were at war. The servant is staggering across the town square carrying an enormous joint of beef.

◄ *The Roast Beef of Old England* or *The Calais Gate* by William Hogarth. The picture is in the Tate Gallery in London.

Food and drink

▲ *Bar at the Folies Bergère* by Edouard Manet. You can see this painting at the Courtauld Institute Galleries in London.

These two pictures show people eating and drinking in bars and cafés in Paris 100 years ago. They were painted by artists who belonged to a group called the Impressionists. They were given this name because they often painted their pictures quickly, catching the 'impression' of sunlight on water or light and shade on people's faces.

Although all the people in the bar on the left seem to be enjoying themselves, the girl serving at the front looks rather bored. The man and woman sitting in the café below, look even more gloomy. They are drinking a strong wine, but it does not seem to be making them feel happy. Perhaps the artist wanted to show how drinking sometimes has bad effects.

◄ *At the Café* by Edgar Degas. This painting is in the Musée d'Orsay in Paris.

The Buckwheat Harvest by Emile Bernard. It is in a private collection in Switzerland.

The picture above, like those on the previous two pages, was also painted by a French artist, but it is a very different subject. This picture, painted at the beginning of the twentieth century, shows a harvest scene. The artist has used strong, bright colours, without any shadows, for his painting of men and women gathering in the corn. The people are wearing the traditional clothes that farm workers wore in France at the turn of the century.

► *Grandma's Hearth Stone* by John Haberle. This picture is in the Detroit Institute of Arts in the USA.

▼ *Campbell's Soup*, a screen print made by Andy Warhol. Wolverhampton Art Gallery, England. © 1995 The Andy Warhol Foundation for the Visual Arts/ARS, New York.

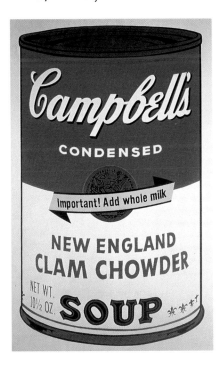

These two pictures come from the USA. The hearth, with simmering pots and all the ornaments, make a warm, cosy scene.

On the left is a tin of soup – a familiar object which you have probably seen in a supermarket. The artist, Andy Warhol, often showed ordinary subjects like this.

Who are the artists?

Giuseppe Arcimboldo (1530-93). This artist lived in Milan, in Italy. He became very famous for painting pictures of people made from fruit, flowers and vegetables. He painted *Winter* on page 5.

Emile Bernard (1868-1941). Bernard was born in France. He was a friend of both Paul Cézanne and Paul Gauguin. and they were all part of a group called the Post-Impressionists. Bernard painted many of his pictures in Brittany, the countryside he has used in his picture *The Buckwheat Harvest*, on page 26.

Pieter Brueghel (the Elder) (c.1525-69). Brueghel was born in the country we now call Belgium. He was the father of two sons, Jan and Pieter, who were also famous painters. You can see his picture *Peasant Wedding* on page 9.

Caravaggio (1573-1609). Caravaggio was born near Milan in Italy. He asked ordinary people who he met in the street to pose as models. His paintings show the contrast of dark shadows and brightly lit areas which give his pictures a lively quality. He was a forceful and rebellious person who met his death during a quarrel, when he was stabbed. His painting *Supper at Emmaus* is on page 4.

Paul Cézanne (1839-1906). Cézanne used some of the ideas of the Impressionist artists, but he wanted to take their ideas further. He became known as one of the leading Post-Impressionist artists ('post' means after), and his work greatly influenced other artists who came after him. His *Still Life with Jug and Fruit* is on page 20.

Pieter Claesz (c.1596-1661). Claesz lived in Holland and specialized in painting still lifes, which he called 'breakfast pieces'. You can see his *Breakfast Still Life with a Crab* on page 19.

Edgar Degas (1834-1917). Degas was one of the Impressionist group of artists. Some of his most famous works are pictures of ballet dancers, cabaret singers and acrobats. His picture *At the Café* is on page 25.

Paul Gauguin (1848-1903). For many years Gauguin worked in a city office, painting only at weekends. When he was thirty-five he went to Brittany, where Emile Bernard also lived. Gauguin painted many pictures in France but later he went to live on an island in the Pacific Ocean, where he also made many paintings. You can see his *Still Life with Mangoes* on page 21.

Vincent van Gogh (1853-90). Van Gogh was born in the Netherlands but painted many of his most famous pictures in France. He studied the work of earlier Dutch artists and enjoyed the work of the Impressionists, many of whom were his friends. His paintings are famous for their brilliant colours and energetic brushwork. His picture *The Potato Eaters* is on page 11.

John Haberle (1858-1933). Haberle was an American, working at the end of the nineteenth and early twentieth centuries. He often painted pictures that would amuse and confuse the viewer, including objects that are not normally part of a picture. His painting *Grandma's Hearth Stone* is on page 27.

William Hogarth (1697-1764). Hogarth was an English artist who lived in London. Although he painted portraits, his most famous pictures are scenes from the lives of ordinary men and women. These pictures often told a story about people's bad behaviour, or about the social problems in England at that time. Although the pictures are amusing, they carry a message about what was right and wrong in people's lives. You can see his *Roast Beef of Old England* on page 23.

Charles van Loo (1705-65). Van Loo lived in France. He had two brothers who were also famous painters working in France. Charles became Principal Painter to the French king, Louis XV. You can see his picture, *La Chasse*, on page 10.

Edouard Manet (1832-83). Manet was one of the leading Impressionist painters. His *Bar at the Folies Bergère*, which you can see on page 24, was his last great work, painted in 1881, a couple of years before he died.

Rembrandt van Rijn (1606-69). Rembrandt was one of the greatest of all Dutch artists. He began his career painting pictures of stories, of Ancient Greece and Rome and from the Bible. Later he made his money from painting portraits of people in Amsterdam, where he lived. He also painted many portraits of himself. You can see his painting *The Flayed Ox*, on page 23.

Jan Vermeer (1632-75). Vermeer was also Dutch. Until this century, many of his works had been almost forgotten, but he is now considered to be one of the world's finest painters. You can see his painting of a kitchenmaid, *The Maid with a Milk Jug*, on page 22.

Andy Warhol (c.1928-87). Warhol was an American artist who was associated with 'Pop Art'. This type of art developed in the 1950s and 1960s, and it made use of comics, films and advertisements. You can see his screen print, *Campbell's Soup*, on page 27.

Glossary

aboriginal   Relating to the native Australian people.

aristocrats   Noblemen and women – people considered to be of superior rank to others.

bagpipes   A wind instrument consisting of a bag and several pipes.

banquet   A large, grand meal for many people, usually held to celebrate a special occasion.

carcass   The dead body of an animal that has been slaughtered (killed) for food.

chariot   An open two-wheeled carriage, normally pulled by horses.

disciples   Followers of a religious teacher, in this instance, Jesus Christ, the founder of Christianity.

dough   Flour that has been moistened and kneaded, ready for baking.

emperor   The ruler of a large group of countries, called an empire.

festive   Joyful and happy, or having to do with a festival.

hampers   Large baskets, often used for carrying food.

hearth   Fireplace.

Impressionists   A group of artists painting at the end of the nineteenth century in France. They recorded their impressions of light and colour in their work.

maize   Also called Indian corn, it is a cereal with large yellow grains, which grow on a spike or cob.

Middle Ages   The period between the end of the Roman Empire and the Renaissance, from about AD 500 to AD 1500.

miracle   A fortunate happening that has no natural cause.

papyrus   A kind of paper made from the stem of a reed, used by the Ancient Egyptians.

ploughing   Turning up the soil in furrows or trenches, ready for seeds to be sown.

relief   A kind of sculpture which is partly three-dimensional. It is usually set against a wall and viewed from one side, like a painting.

thresh   To separate grain from straw by beating it.

traditional   According to custom.

vegetarians   People who eat only vegetable foods, and do not eat meat.

Books to read

The Book of Art – A Way of Seeing (Ernest Benn, 1979).

Every Picture Tells a Story by Rolf Harris (Phaidon, 1989).

Food – through the eyes of artists by Wendy and Jack Richardson (Macmillan, 1991).

History Through Art series (Wayland, 1995).

Just Look... A Book about Paintings by Robert Cumming (Viking Kestrel, 1986).

About the pictures in this book

Of course, all the pictures in this book are photographs. Some, like the relief on page 8 and the clay pots on page 12, show the works exactly as the artist made them. But remember that looking at a photograph of a painting is not the same as seeing the painting itself. If possible you should try to visit a picture gallery or museum, where you may be able to find pictures and decorated objects showing food or people eating, or models and carvings of various foods. Why not make a still life of some food, like the pictures on pages 18 to 21, or a model of fruit or cakes?

Picture acknowledgements
The publishers have attempted to contact all copyright holders of the illustrations in this title, and apologise if there have been any oversights.
The photographs in this book were supplied by: Bridgeman Art Library *cover* (top left, top right), 4, 5, 9, 10, 11, 19, 20, 21, 22, 23 (top), 24, 25, 27 (both); Michael Holford © 6 (top), 7, 15 (lower); Ronald Sheridan Ancient Art and Architecture Library 8 (both), 16 (both), 17; Tate Gallery 23 (lower); Wayland Picture Library *cover* (bottom left), 26; Werner Forman Archive *cover* (bottom right), 6 (lower), 12, 13 (both), 14, 15 (top), 18. *Campbell's Soup* by Andy Warhol on page 27 appears by permission of the copyright holders © 1995 The Andy Warhol Foundation for the Visual Arts/ARS, New York.

Index

ancient works of art
  Chinese 14
  Egyptian 6
  Greek 7
  Roman 8, 18
  South American 12
Arcimboldo, Giuseppe 5, 28
Australia 13

bark painting 13
Bernard, Emile 26, 28
Brueghel, Pieter the Elder 9, 28

cafés 24, 25
Caravaggio 4, 28
Cézanne, Paul 20, 28
Claesz, Pieter 19, 28

Degas, Edgar 25, 28

farming 6, 16, 26
feasts 9, 16, 17
fruit 5, 18, 19, 20, 21

Gauguin, Paul 21, 28
Gogh, Vincent van 11, 29

Haberle, John 27, 29
harvest 16, 26
Hogarth, William 23, 29

Impressionists 24, 30

kitchens 6, 22

Japan 15

Loo, Charles van 10, 29

Manet, Edouard 24, 29
meat 15, 23
Middle Ages 16-17

North America 13

paintings
  A Banquet and Concert 14
  At the Café 25
  Bar at the Folies Bergère 24
  Breakfast Still Life with a Crab 19
  The Buckwheat Harvest 26
  The Flayed Ox 23
  Grandma's Hearth Stone 27
  La Chasse 10
  The Maid with a Milk Jug 22
  The Marriage of Cana 16
  The Roast Beef of Old England 23
  Peasant Wedding 9
  The Potato Eaters 11
  Still Life with Jug and Fruit 20
  Still Life with Mangoes 21
  Supper at Emmaus 4
  Winter 5

Rembrandt 23, 29

screen print 27
sculpture 8

Vermeer, Jan 22, 29
vegetables 5, 11

wall paintings 6, 8, 18
Warhol, Andy 27, 29
weddings 9, 16, 17